BEFORE THEY START

TO LEAVE

BEFORE THEY START TO LEAVE

For Parents of Teen-Agers —
Some Quiet Directions

WALTER RIESS

CONCORDIA PUBLISHING HOUSE
SAINT LOUIS

Concordia Publishing House, St. Louis, Missouri
Concordia Publishing House Ltd., London, E. C. 1
© 1967 Concordia Publishing House
Library of Congress Catalog No. 67-22998

For my parents
always in a ministry

For on a strong hill, O Eternal One,
Thou hadst set me by Thy favor

David

Psalm 30:7 (Moffatt)

When to the sessions of sweet silent thought
I summon up remembrance of things past

William Shakespeare

Sonnet XXX

Contents

Author's Note   9

Self-Discovery: The Spiritual Problem of Our
    Teen-Agers   11

His Holy Spirit: A Resolution for Teen-Agers   15

Adolescence: The New Birth in the Spirit   19

As We Love Ourselves   23

Why the Church Loses Teen-Agers   27

But How Do You Reach Your Own?   31

The Walls of Glass Between Us   35

When the Walls Come Tumbling Down   40

"I Will Have Compassion"   45

The Techniques of Our Compassion   49

When We Fail   55

The Leaving of a Heritage   59

A Teen-Age Hope for Oneness   64

Tell Us: We Are Never Alone   69

The Risk unto Life: Youth Leading the Church   74

The Size of Teen-Age Life   79

The Young Church Is *for Us*   85

Toward Power in Their World   90

Author's Note

This book does not attempt to present an analysis of all the psychophysical relationships of adolescence or of the complex and highly charged high school world in which our adolescents live.

I want to offer instead a positive spiritual approach to the massive changes going on inside and outside our teen-agers — and a motivation in faith for confronting these changes boldly within the fellowship of the home and the church. I am convinced that only such a confrontation, in such a fellowship, can possibly give our youth the desire and will — and insight into their own self-value — to keep growing in the stature of our Lord Jesus Christ.

WR

Self-Discovery:
The Spiritual Problem of
Our Teen-Agers

I have known teen-agers too long not to realize how intensely—and sometimes how fiercely—they wrestle for a sense of meaning in their personalities and lives.

A girl of 16, trying to find herself as a writer, said in my office, "If I don't make a go of this, *I'll never have a happy day in my life.*" Writing was the one gift she had discovered in herself, and she just may have been telling the truth about her future. For her writing *was* her meaning—so far her only meaning. And she clung to that meaning with all the ferocity of a cornered and threatened tigress.

The stuff in teen-agers, even Christian teen-agers, that lashes out at adults with resentment, hostility, and destruction often stems from this same fierce search for personal meaning. The teen-ager who feels that he's losing out in his search may project his frustration and despair onto the person who can most conveniently be blamed for the failure. Usually that person is the parent of the opposite sex, sometimes a teacher, sometimes a representative of the law, and sometimes all of them.

But the question quickly becomes obvious. How can all the teen-agers in a generation conceived after a world war—all the unsettled youth for whom we can find neither employment nor education enough—possibly find a driving and dynamic meaning in their individual lives? Can any person or agency (including the church) possibly help each teen-ager find this meaning without which a growing personality and life becomes impossible?

This is the question that now puzzles and threatens our educational agencies, our government programs for youth, and our church outreach to teen-agers. It is a question so terrifying—even in the *possibility* of a negative answer—that most of us would much rather run away from all confrontation with teen-agers and teen-age groups and simply not ask the thing at all.

But I think the question has to be asked. I think we Christians have to do the asking. I think we alone can dive down into the depths and come up with the jewel that is the answer.

Why? Because the answer is spiritual, not social or psychic, in nature.

Personal self-discovery, in the view of the Christian pastor and teacher, has always been a bit of a jigsaw puzzle to put together in any pulpit or on any platform.

You can tell a teen-ager he is at once a sinner and a saved person, and the teen-ager will nod at you in quiet agreement. You can tell him that sanctification is a process of growing in grace and the grace of living, and there is still no argument. But the question still hangs in the air: What does all this mean about my personality, my gifts, my use of my gifts, my personal calling, my inner drive toward my mission, right here and now?

All this calls for much more of an answer than many of us can possibly give. Our teen-agers' quest for personal self-discovery meanwhile and perhaps endlessly goes frustrated and unanswered. And it isn't only the teen-ager who is frustrated. All of us—Christian adults trying desperately to fill the void we sense in the lives of our young people—sense their disappointment in us, and as often as not we end up blaming ourselves for losing a battle we had no weapons to fight in the first place.

This battle will not go to the same old answers with the same old authority behind the answers. The old answers won't do, as we're finding out rather painfully in the statistics of delinquency, illegitimate births, and police records even among suburban, white, Anglo-Saxon, Protestant, well-bred adolescents. Somewhere along the adolescent line there has to be a fresh and vigorous rediscovery of a personal relationship to the Holy Spirit, a rediscovery of a personal relationship that will pour a fresh and vigorous *sense of calling* into the heart of a youth. Otherwise that heart will remain a heart of darkness in a time of disjointed and confusing ideologies.

I believe that rediscovery of a personal relationship to the Holy Spirit can happen to a teen-ager. More than that, I believe we — Christian parents, teachers, youth leaders, the concerned ones — can set the stage for it. And I believe that we can come to view this setting of the stage as our highest accent in our contact with our teen-agers — in the home, in the school, and in the church.

We do not really have much of a choice. The time is past or very near past when we shall be able to hold or even interest our teen-agers in the milky entertainment of past youth programs or in the purely catechetical approach to the teachings of the church. Make no mistake about it, high school youth have engaged themselves in the tug and push of too many really revolutionary movements to get excited any longer over a weak call to mere veneration of old truths. We cannot get away with that any longer — and I, for one, think this is one of the best things that has happened to the church in a long time.

Now we are forced to do the creative job of coming to our teen-agers, not with the dry husks of past reapings but with the real *essence* of our life with God. What *is* that essence? What *is* that relationship about which we talk so long inside ourselves and often so little outside ourselves? Can we communicate *this* to our teen-agers?

I think we can.

But I think we have to start talking first-person singular, active voice, present tense—about the Holy Spirit.

His Holy Spirit:
A Resolution for
Teen-Agers

I come to any lines about the Holy Spirit in teen-age lives with a strange and undeniable inner draw to the subject. I think this is because my personal experience in my own adolescence forces me to the conclusion that the Holy Spirit *is* a resolution to the problems of the high school years.

I remember too well what my discovery of a *living* Holy Spirit, born of a living grasp on the Gospel of Jesus Christ, meant to me and in me in the days when wonderment—and terror—about the meaning of my own self grew long and deep. I remember that, for me, living in the Holy Spirit suddenly became a possibility, then a reality. I remember praying far into the night, and through hours of walking in days of endless opening, for the life of the Holy Spirit that I knew lay just ahead of me.

I remember how the truth came over me—the reality that living in the Holy Spirit means living in a perpetual awareness that a miracle of growing and healing may happen even in a teen-ager, any time, any day, every day.

I remember, still with a bittersweet surge of awareness, my awakening to the fact that I was not alone, that I was never alone, that instead I (even a teen-ager) was gifted with the support and the all-surrounding power of a really resurrected and acting and planning Lord Christ, Savior and King in reality of all creation.

I remember discovering that living in the Holy Spirit meant calling on His power even in the little laughable things that bring so much delight — and sometimes so much pain — into our high school days.

I remember discovering that living in the Holy Spirit meant living in prayer, acting in a sense of constant prayer, making decisions and carrying on the work of communicating faith to other teen-agers in the immense certainty of inner prayer.

I remember my surprise at finding all this power, and all this joy, deep in the heart of the church faith I had inherited from a white, wooden parsonage deep enough in the bowels of Detroit to feel the steady threat of poverty and neighborhood tensions.

Now when I meet with my teen-age discussion group, on any given Sunday morning, and hear their confusion and puzzlement and somtimes panic over the temptations they are facing, of the doubts battering them in some science course, I keep wondering how to communicate adequately how very real this Holy Spirit is, how ready He is to enter their consciousness as well as their church and sacramental life, and how the experience of becoming conscious of His meaning and His guidance can indeed help them face those high school hours that are most terrifying and yet most exhilarating.

How do you say this to teen-agers? How do you say it without sounding sensational or maudlin or as if you were trying to sell them a holy-holy way of life that will alienate them from every friend they have?

I think there are basically only two ways open to us.

The first way is to *be* the kind of persons ourselves who are not holy-holy or antihuman but rather human and real and alive to the deepest fibers of our being.

The second is to be willing to tell, honestly and humbly and without embarrassment, the story of *how* the Holy

Spirit came to mean so much to us and *how* our consciousness of Him did really change life for us—and made life a story of faith and victory instead of defeat and fear.

All of this implies, of course, that we shall tell also of the rich inner streams feeding this life in the Holy Spirit— the Gospel, the sacraments, the prayers of the Psalms, the witness of all the saints around us, the encouragement and the patience of that solitary congregation where we bring our weekly burden into worship and fellowship. I am conscious that this too can come out wrong, can drive teen-agers away from listening and away from a life in the Holy Spirit. And so all of it must be said with a genuineness and an insight into the nature of high school youth as well as with a confidence in the Holy Spirit Himself.

The point is that the whole matter of the Holy Spirit has to be put to our teen-agers one way or the other. The thing has to be said. For in the teen-age years nothing less than the centrality and the guidance and the dynamic of the Holy Spirit will do. I say this from personal experience and from my own efforts to find a lot of other less-than-spiritual answers to the full gamut of adolescent perplexities that rose inside and outside me in my own high school experience.

So often, I am afraid, the church has said less than the full meaning of the Holy Spirit—to teen-agers *and* to adults—simply because of embarrassment or because of an inbuilt inferiority feeling, to wit: *Yes, in the church we do have our answers, but outside the faith of the church there are answers too. And who knows whether these may not be better, finer, more accurate answers in the long run?*

This sense of possible inferiority to someone or something else's way of life communicates itself to our youth. I am convinced that many of them leave the church *for* the imagined finer shores of some other kind of life simply because they sense *inside* the church that self-doubt that only adds to the inner confusion of their adolescence. What we so often hold out to teen-agers is only a mirror to what they already feel going on deep inside themselves: the gritty reflection of our own terror and our own accusation against our own faith.

This is not quite enough.

What is enough is the total faith that is in ourselves, the total of all our experiences of life through our faith in Jesus Christ, and the total insight into His Spirit that we have come to hold.

What is enough is all this, and the prayer that what we have felt and lived through and found to be our finest and final truth will catch fire in the teen-age breast and send that life into power and love and new meaning in the world.

Adolescence:
the New Birth in
the Spirit

"Adolescence" almost always is said as a word of biology or of sociology (sometimes in a most threatening way) or of mental or emotional pathology. It is a word we have come to speak most easily when we are talking about riots in the street or trouble in the home or panty raids or psychiatrists' offices. It is not a word we like to mention in churches or in any atmosphere where our concept of God is preeminent.

Yet that is precisely where the word most belongs. For of all the growth and change that sweeps over the human soul in adolescence, most certainly it is the change in *spirit*, in religious—ultimately religious—interest and drives, that unites all the pulls and pressures of these years into a meaningful whole that can be grappled with.

My own realization of this stems not so much from the vague tinges of theological insight occurring in some rare works on the psychology of adolescence. Rather I am convinced by the almost phenomenal reorientation of personality and character in hundreds of Christian adolescents I have known and counseled, that the deepest and most intense crisis of adolescence is spiritual—and nothing else or less. And we have so often done our youth less than a service in relegating their very real struggles of spirit to the shelf of biology and the purely physical sciences.

In my experience these struggles can indeed lead to the higher unity so much and so long sought by adolescents. I have seen striking and swift reorganization of the self take place in many Christian teen-agers.

I will go even farther. I will say that *absence* of this spiritual struggle for the life in the Holy Spirit, this religious quest for a new unity of the soul with God, means that growth is *not* taking place. If the teen-age personality does not wrestle for a whole life with Jesus Christ, there is an arresting of development, a frustration of God's purpose for that life, and so a frustration of that life for life itself, even on purely human terms.

Some years ago I served as counselor in a camp of 60 Christian high school students and listened while the leaders compared their Christian experiences among themselves, each one of them testifying to His power in day-by-day living. When it was all over, one of the young teen-age boys said to me: "I never knew religion could be so exciting. I never knew all this was there for me!"

By "this" he meant the thrill of sensing a new orientation within himself—an orientation in Jesus Christ as Savior of the world, an orientation blessed and stimulated by the felt presence of the Holy Spirit.

Most of the young campers, judging from their response, went home different people. They had come to a vision of the Spirit at work in their lives. They knew now what they *could have* in life with their Lord. And they sensed, perhaps even unconsciously, that this possibility alone completely changed the picture of life that they had so far learned to accept and live with and for—if somewhat questioningly.

It is hard to write about this experience without seeming to exaggerate either its universality or its effectiveness. I am fully aware that not all youth seem open to the radical resetting of their personalities that emerges from a new consciousness of the real presence of Jesus Christ in their world and their lives and the real flowing of the power of the Holy Spirit through their lives. I am also aware, however, that the experience has taken almost visible shape in very many situations where a youth counselor has had the courage and patience and humility to present the case *for* the Holy Spirit. And I *have* seen teen-age lives changed with an almost incredible swiftness and power.

Most of us, at one time or another, have felt this immense nearness of our Lord — His openness to our outreach and our cry — that may strike some teen-agers full force at a camp retreat or in some quiet moment in a cathedral. We have experienced that sudden lightning stroke that lights up the whole sky around us and in us and fills us with the joy and security of seeing ourselves completely surrounded by the love of Jesus Christ. It is quite possible that we have written off the experience as a moment of passion — something akin to falling in love at first sight or seeing Niagara Falls at night on a honeymoon trip.

But the truth is that we are dealing with a force far higher than all this. We are confronting a power that has reintegrated the young human personality and pulled the pieces of adolescence together and given fresh new impetus to a young life perplexed by its own crises and can still do so.

There are always means, of course. The revitalization of the Spirit of God still dwells immensely — and very practically — in the Gospel, in Holy Communion, in Baptism, in the preaching of the Good News in the church.

But we dare not allow the commonness and ready availability of the *means* to blind us to the true miracle and life-redeeming character of the thing that can happen, and does, in adolescence.

There is nothing common about the rebirth of a person. And adolescence is almost nothing but a lost weekend without the rebirth, a gift of the Holy Spirit, sent by Jesus Christ, who is Himself present in our lives as a gift of the Father in heaven.

For adolescence is *His best time* to do the miracle of rebirth, of reintegration, of resurrection.

In fact, for some lives and some persons there may be no other time.

As We Love
Ourselves

A few weeks ago a boy in one of our church high schools wrote me in mournful terms about his rather exaggerated sins of dating one particular girl too steadily and risking some typical adventures against dormitory rules. He wasn't exactly the greatest sinner in the high school world (even though he thought so), and I told him that.

I also told him that he sure could become what he *thought* he was if he kept on running himself down this way.

I knew what I was talking about. When I was in high school I let the general atmosphere of the place — including the ribbing of my classmates — convince me that being thin and tall made me ugly as sin. If fact, I would gladly have traded my 155 pounds of 6-foot-4 for any good old-fashioned sin. Instead I lived under the constant temptation simply to run myself into the ground, and I didn't dream that this temptation was as bad as any that could come to a teen-age boy. But it *was*.

It was a real inner conviction, this despairing of the work that the Holy Spirit could do in a gangly boy of 6-foot-4 and 155 pounds, complete with pimples and frame glasses and pants that never kept growing with long adolescent legs. The truth was that, while I prayed for God's gifts of love, I despaired of the capacity of my body, mind, and spirit to receive His gifts. The truth was that I almost despaired of the whole process of getting that body, mind, and spirit through the high school years.

But all this inner conviction became quickly habitual, and almost a denial of the grace of the Lord already given to me. My Baptism, my attendance to the Gospel and the Sacrament of the Altar, did not seem to change the course of self-accusation and self-condemnation. I lived in perpetual terror that absolutely no givenness of God Himself could possibly make my adolescent frame and its agonies of growing up worth the while.

How much I would have given then for a voice to tell me that adolescence (even for a Christian boy) *is* long legs and thin arms and pimples and stumbling. How much more for a counselor who could have said, in quiet acceptance of me, that I would not soon be able to love anybody else unless I came to love myself—at least a little! How much for a Christ-minded teacher who might have breathed into my life then the insight that it could not be wrong to love that same self created, redeemed, and renewed totally by the Holy Spirit!

But always it is terribly hard to accept our teen-agers this way, with any degree of spiritual insight and encouragement. And some teen-agers do act so obnoxious in the process of growing up and through the high school years that we simply cannot leap over the barriers that their obstinacy throws up between us. I can remember a high school teacher handing me some little metal first award for winning a table-tennis tournament. For a moment the wall came tumbling down—and then my embarrassed, awkward smile brought it up again. He said, "I'm sure it was a great victory," or something on that order. But if he hadn't said it, if he had only given a look of acceptance and encouragement that day, I might very well have gone to him that same evening for some spiritual help.

Now, when even Christian teen-agers speak or act in ways that I cannot understand, I try to catch my anger and resentment in my teeth, and I try to listen and watch. In some inner place I will always be conscious of the fact that the Holy Spirit's presence does not automatically reverse the deep, sharp scarrings of the green years. And teen-agers deprived of prayers and love and acceptance cannot simply outgrow their disadvantages by sheer force of the Holy Spirit. For He comes and He works in teen-agers through other people — and sometimes, tragically, they aren't *there*.

What more important business can the church of Jesus Christ have than reinsulating the love-deprived and the loneliness-scarred teen-agers among us? What mission of the church can outrank this in importance? What can be more vital than that we who are in Jesus Christ by the power of His Holy Spirit so love our young girls and boys that they finally arrive even at that point *where they can love themselves?*

For until this happens, this capacity to love their own bodies, their own minds, and their own spirits, they will not be able to love anybody else — adults or church or community or teachers or youth groups. Until a teen-ager can say, "I believe that my Lord has created and redeemed and refreshed in me a unique and deep and meaningful personality and life," we have no right to expect any other response *but* confusion and resentment from these priceless spirits.

But saying any of this, or all of this, is saying that the Holy Spirit has been brought to bear upon some teen-agers *through the conscious effort and love of the church*. And this conscious effort and love for youth is both the gift and the direction of the Holy Spirit Himself. The circle is complete when, in His endless care for and outpouring upon our teen-agers, He carries them into that mature frame wherein they themselves may care for and love and accept and build others whom the Lord leads to them.

This is the way the Holy Spirit does operate in the youth program of the church: through the earthy and earth-bound love of persons who are by no means always sure of their way of working but are nevertheless concerned to the point of tears about the teen-agers whom the blessed Lord Jesus Christ surrounds with His dying and resurrected love.

Why the Church Loses
Teen-Agers

A consciousness of the Holy Spirit comes to teen-agers through the speaking of the Gospel of Jesus Christ—this tremendous power inherent in His life, sacrifice, death, resurrection, and presence with us—and through His sacraments of Baptism and the Altar, the visible gifts of His hold on us and His life in us.

But note that none of this *can* come to teen-agers without the love of the people around teen-agers. Obviously, adolescents do not naturally tell Gospel to each other, and they cannot give the Sacrament to each other. For any of this and all of this they call for love—the love of the church, the love of adults who will guarantee to them and for them, by the power of the Spirit, the meaning and presence of Jesus Christ, sent by the Father in heaven to be the Bridegroom of the church.

When Christians fail to act as guarantors of this meaning and Presence, the life of the teen-ager and the life of of the church itself are both short-circuited.

A young girl, burdened enough by worries of loneliness and despair to come with her father to my church office one summer evening, confessed that she had never before that night prayed with a pastor anywhere, anytime. We knelt, the three of us, before the rich wood of that altar under the soaring stone arches of the chancel, in light so dim that we could scarcely see, had we looked upward, the high reaches of the saints and angels carved into the oak. And into that darkness there did come a certainty that our Savior would indeed help—as He proved when the girl, a year or so later, was found by and married to a Christian young man who permanently ended her fears of being forever alone.

But I could not at the time miss seeing the tragedy in the situation—that a girl of 19, born and reared in the fellowship of the Lord's people, under the care and guidance of a stream of persons and in the enjoyment of church youth groups for over 7 years, had never once received the support, the guarantee, of prayer with a pastor. I doubt very much, in fact, whether she had prayed alone with any other person in that church in all those 19 years. No wonder she felt alone and afraid and terrified by the future!

Her panic might as well have driven her completely out of the church. And then some minor statistic might record the fact that another confirmand "drifted" from the faith—drifted like so many of those incorrigible, unreachable, rebellious adolescents, those irresponsible teen-agers who have no real place or purpose in a well-organized congregation.

I was reminded of this altar prayer again at an Ozark mountain resort, where in the recent past I met with 20 young people for two days of recreation-program work for Missouri churches and, on the second morning, a service of Holy Communion in which all of us became keenly aware of the mystery and potential of our being so together in the Holy Spirit. After two days of close, warm friendship and mutual confessing of self to one another, the Sacrament seemed a climaxing benediction of our Christ upon our being together. Then again the same question haunted me, as I'm sure it rose in the minds of those who worshiped there: *Why has this not happened before to us? Why is our church so slow, so reluctant, so doubtful, to cry out its breath and its purpose in breathing by exactly this kind of sacramental person-to-person giving of self?*

Where, in our crowded time and places, will we find the answer to why we have so largely deserted our own breaking of bread and prayers together and abandoned our own teen-agers to a spiritual search too often deprived of help and as lonely as a ship at night? Do we distrust the miracle of presence that the Creator Spirit has shined on us, or the body and blood that rest on our own tongues, or the Word of love and forgiveness that pours over our own heads, so that we are ashamed to pour forth what we ourselves can hardly believe to be real? Or have we traded all the immediacy of the Gospel of our Christ and the vitality of His Spirit for a list of secondhand principles and programs, lifeless in themselves but able to keep our churches at least in motion if not in power? Or have we ourselves never really been reached and surrounded and sent into mission by others—perhaps by adults whom *we* loved when *we* were teen-agers and whose longing to praise the name of the Lamb of God would not quite let them keep silent about Him?

It will not help us, if any of this is true, to know all the psychology of adolescence in the Library of Congress or to be able to speak in the calypso slang of the high school years or to approach teen-agers with the zippy and clever questions of tracts that "zero in on their problems." So often the church, as an unchurched writer friend of mine puts it, seems to be running after the world like a monk with his cowl pulled tight around him, desperately trying to keep up with the pace and glibness of those *who have already given up hope.* The real problem of adolescence is to be found far beneath all this jargon and gimmickry.

I saw a lot of the problem solved, or at least partly resolved, in the eyes of the young persons who communed at that resort camp table-altar, in the hope visible in the face of one 19-year-old girl after one chancel prayer that summer night, and in a letter from six teen-age boys who said they were going to try to become ministers — all because a single experience of worship had convinced them there was more excitement in living in Jesus Christ than in racing motorcycles through the streets of a Florida town.

But this kind of commitment, this depth of dedication and rededication, stems from those rare moments when the church suddenly becomes the church and the power of God's love in us flashes among us like some strange lightning. And so we have to talk of such commitment in awed tones — and only the statistics of *loss* of youth to the churches receive the regular publicity and the normal acceptance of common report.

Shouldn't it all be the other way around? "My sheep *hear* My voice, and I *know* them, and they *follow* Me, and I *give* unto them eternal life." And that 70 percent of youth who seem not to hear His voice, who seem not to follow, who do not get gathered up into the Eternal Arms, are the ones to be awed about.

They are too alone to care. And maybe we are too ashamed of our Gospel to touch them.

And our Lord has no hands to touch them but our hands, however shaky and uncertain they are. *These* are His hands. It is a terrible, and a joyful, thing to remember when we talk with our adolescents.

Best of all, it is a thing that can take at least some of the shame and some of the fear from our voices. Even when we recite the statistics of our losses of our own warmest promise of the church tomorrow, our Christian teen-agers.

For really now, could the statistics hold up against His touch in our hands, if we dare to reach out to our own children even in our own weakness?

But How Do You
Reach Your Own?

It is always an extremely difficult business to write of the Holy Spirit, who remains so infinitely and so patiently out of the reach of our words. I am reminded of John F. Kennedy's consideration that the most appropriate lines in William Shakespeare were, for him at least—

GLENDOWER: I can call spirits from the vasty deep.
HOTSPUR: Why, so can I, or so can any man,
            But will they come when you do call for
            them?

I Henry IV, III, i

But it is possible for any of us to fail to see that in the higher order of the Christian Gospel the Holy Spirit always *does* come in all and to all the invocations that we bring to Him. Indeed, the sheer reminding of each other that we do in awareness of His presence is enough power and object in itself for one life.

It is important for us to remember this even when we confront our own children. With them, too, we deal in that so-cheap commodity of words. And among the millions of words we speak with them and at them in our years of rearing teen-agers, the words *Jesus Christ* and *Holy Spirit* and *forgiveness* and *acceptance* and *renewing* may seem quite trivial—so trivial, in fact, that we would do as well to forget them and get on with the more real facts of living.

Added to this is the truth that family intimacy does not make easier in the least the mention of our Lord's name or the discussion of His significance in our home. It is in many ways much simpler for me to preach Gospel to thousands than to say one word of His grace to my own daughters.

Yet I cannot help but realize that only a *word* about His grace can make my day with these daughters worth the remembering. I stand in the same relationship to them as to the people of my church; it is my Christian obligation—my trust—to *speak* the words that spell out to my own children, in no uncertain terms: *You are not alone. The Holy Spirit* is *the Lord also of your life, as He is of mine. You are one of the redeemed ones, and I am too, and together we are the church. We may be the church only in this house, but we* are *the church of Jesus Christ, and His Spirit* is *with us.*

This kind of thing is power.

And it can be done in all sorts of ways. In our home we end each evening dinner by singing a West Indies arrangement of the Lord's Prayer to the accompaniment of a ukelele strummed (sometimes much too energetically) by our young teen daughter. Night offers the opportunity to stand as a family around each bed and sing a child's hymn such as "Jesus, Gentle Shepherd" or "Jesus Loves Me" or only to say with each other a simple benediction or child's prayer. And the next morning, before our young teen-ager runs out for school, there is a moment's breath to call out: "I'll say a prayer for you. Have a good day!"

They're small words, often not answered, seemingly not heard, possibly not heeded. And then one day over the long distance phone I listened while my young teen-ager told me: "I'm praying for you, Daddy, so I know you'll have a good meeting!" And those few words would have made that meeting "good" had it been held in Hades.

The words do not come glibly, I know. They come only with all the force of will we can build up through years of Christian marriage and homelife. But those *words* are really the way we can reinforce each other in the life of the Holy Spirit. They are the way we can make our stand for the lordship of Jesus Christ over our life.

I do not mean to imply that words are the only way for us to witness to the supremacy of the Holy Spirit in our homes. In a sense, every action that takes place in our family living witnesses, positively or negatively, to His depth in our common days.

To act *for* Him in our homes is to love, accept, and forgive even our own children—even our teen-agers! To act *for* Him in our churches is to forgive even those hideous sins which, because of their unforgettable qualities, keep reminding us of our own failures as parents every day of our lives: the babies without fathers, without the sanction of legitimacy, without the sanction even of our own healed consciences.

And if one of those unforgettable transgressions should take place in our own family, to act *for* Christ is to bow our head humbly beneath the new yoke of pain and grief and to say to the one who has transgressed: "This does not change my love for you. *I am human enough to be filled with anxiety and tears about what you have done, and what I have failed to do for you, but I have enough of the Holy Spirit of Christ with me to forgive in the midst of my anxiety and tears.*"

In a very real sense, this is the only way the church can go on existing. For if there is one disillusionment that comes with being Christian, it is to learn that we are still what we are, we are still what we were from the bed of conception, from the all-too-failing flesh and blood of our own fathers and our own mothers, who formed the church of their own time.

So we are here as failures in our own right. Yet we are here. Yet we are the church.

And the Spirit of Jesus Christ is encompassed by the width of our vision, born of such flesh and blood. And in the center of our vision, whatever it is, are our children.

The Walls of Glass
Between Us

The church, to teen-agers, resembles nothing so much as a maze of puzzling walls, something like a weird hall of mirrors in a county-fair fun house. You can walk right in, and there is even a welcome from a man at the door. But there the welcome ends, and the frustration of search begins. The walls are the thick glass of adult concepts and adult frozenness, and the maze of them is endless. It is possible to wander for years without finding that one single point of communication that suddenly brings "church" to life in the adolescent consciousness. I have heard from high school youth that not once in all their church relationships did anyone relate the name of Jesus Christ meaningfully to their life experiences.

They do not mean this as an indictment of the church. Far from it, they are actually seeking *for* the church they so desperately need and we find it so hard to provide for them: *that church where the person and life of Father, Son, and Holy Spirit really do move into the teen-age personality as an integrating and maturing power capable of the day-to-day restoring so vital to adolescence.*

There are reasons for the maze of thick glass walls separating our youth from this experience of the church of the Holy Spirit. And these reasons, these hazards, are not of our own making. They are built in by the nature of adolescence (as a phenomenon distinct from other periods of human growth) and of adulthood (as an experience that largely cancels out all memory of the adolescent years, partly for the sake of preserving the adult self-image).

It may be a bit painful to take a look at the wall builders in the church, but we might do well to face the maze that cuts us off from mutual witness with our teen-agers.

The name Jesus Christ means one thing to adults and quite another to teen-agers. To us adults He means the continuing force of redemption and sanctification, especially as these are manifest in the stability of our homes, our work abilities, our social relationships in community and congregational activity, and our hope for eternal life after death. But to the teen-ager, this same name means facing life as an adventure, a commitment to some as yet undiscovered purpose, a dedication to expression of some mystic and utterly potent inner yearning to *be* and to be uniquely *self.* The image and worship of Jesus Christ, it is easy to see, can most effectively give force to this total inner drive.

Doctrinal constructs of any kind are by their very nature foreign to the experience of being a teen-ager. For an adult a doctrinal framework, such as the cycle of creation, redemption, and the office of the keys, and the prooftext system of supporting this framework offer a reassuring background for faith. To a teen-ager, who longs for a less structured and constantly fresh experience of life, such systems may come to violate that sense of inner flow and movement which accompany growing and discovering. Systems of any kind tend overmuch to establish the *status quo* instead of encouraging the radical and God-given search for new and visionary forms of living, creating, expressing, adventuring.

Adult speaking itself tends to take on the form of status quo *acceptance which can violate the instinctive inner longings of a Christian teen-ager.* As we live on in the church, there is no tendency quite so powerful in us as to concretize our wisdom and experience in our speech itself — and even in our worship. So our liturgies and our communications, our friendships and our attitudes, take on a consistency of appearance, a glossy patina quite appealing to other adults but not to teen-agers caught up in the undeniable currents of their own yearnings to *experience.* The teen-ager may do us the favor of calling us "square" (or something worse) and so shake us into feeling some of the force of the currents pulsing through him. Or he may just turn off his inner ear and shut out the sound of our voice. And then he may quietly wrap up his tent and steal away, while we wonder where the little Arabs of the church have gone and why and what we can do to bring them back.

Being accepted by his own kind means so much to our teen-agers that the acceptance of adults in the church can actually threaten him. The exploitation of the adolescent, by people who want the teen-ager's dollar — which is on the verge of controlling 30 percent of the American market — has built up a "culture," a mania for being accepted as and *staying* a teen-ager. So marvelous is this desire to stay a teen-ager that *Seventeen,* a magazine originally published for teen-agers, has come to be classed as a woman's fashion magazine in fashion trade journals.

Acceptance by the peer group, when carried to such a ridiculous extreme, may almost cancel out the normal interrelationships that before World War II (when so much of this started to happen) more or less characterized our church life. The truth is that if you *do* succeed in breaking through to your teen-age fellow Christian, you may find yourself rejected again if other members of your teen-ager's group do not accept you *as a group.*

The alienation of guilt works with the highest force in the adolescent "green years." Every yearning a boy has for a girl, and a girl for a boy, carries with it emotions possibly loaded with self-guilt. This is not just because of a Puritan streak in our church attitudes about sex or because "the kids are really doing things they shouldn't." The truth is that every such adolescent yearning does open up the sudden inner realization not put into so many words: *I am faced with a strange new power in myself. I don't know where it will take me or what damage it may do. Therefore, how in God's name can I be sure it is a* good *power, a redeemed power, a creating and not a destroying power?*

This kind of question, self-doubt, and self-guilt stands behind the shy boy's unwillingness to ask *any* girl for a date. And it stands behind a girl's unwillingness to accept any handholding from any boy. And of course the same self-guilt stands as one of the thick glass walls between girl or boy and the daily Word of grace from and in the church.

The Gospel itself can seem *to the teen-ager to be a power hostile to himself,* who wants to go out and adventure and save the world all by himself. It can seem a dreary and depressing fact to him that Christ has *already* saved the world, particularly if this Gospel message takes such a static form in the local pulpit that there can be no further challenge to new ministry and new forms of exploring the life of adventure and service.

It is no accident that in so few years the Peace Corps of America has captivated so many of the finest spirits among our youth. For the Peace Corps calls upon the young to be saviors, servants, ambassadors to the underdogs of the world. But so often in the church the Word of the Gospel—the Christ who died once for all—has been given to appear as the Grand Finish to all human effort for *any* of the underdogs.

This is why some churches can still ignore the races or the classes that at the moment seem to be composed of "undesirable people." And yet the teen-agers, perhaps out of a feeling of innate sympathy and understanding of what it means to be so treated, want to and would take an amazing role in the church as it still "saves," under the Gospel of Jesus Christ and in the power of the Creator Spirit, the beaten ones who call for its help.

The thick glass walls are even thicker than we had feared. But the Holy Spirit is no respecter at all of walls. They can come crumbling down — and they do.

When the Walls
Come Tumbling Down

It is quite easy to start thinking, in the face of all the walls that do separate our teen-agers from us (and us from each other), that all of us have become simply helpless victims of the walls. And this feeling runs through so much of our attitudes toward our youth that they soon enough accept the role we seem to want them to play — the role of outside critic, rebel without a church, even destroyer of the Christian home.

Such an estimate of the situation, however, points more to a want of faith and hope than to an actual social condition, even in our adolescent-conscious American culture. Because of the reality of the Holy Spirit, the church always remains at least potentially able to break down her own inner walls and has done so usually at that point in time when her own critics were already hauling out their shovels to bury her alive, with her inhibitions intact. Even in our own home, my wife and I have noted that the revival and reopening of channels between our teen-age daughter and ourselves comes often exactly when both she and we have almost given up hope of ever reaching an understanding.

There is a clue in this, and the clue is in the terror and near despair of being human — and accepting ourselves as being only human beggars under the outpouring love and decision of the Father and Son, through the Holy Spirit. We ought to know that we make very poor gods, and our teen-agers know it better than we do. And when we finally grow frustrated enough to think of giving up trying to play God, our humanness starts to show through enough to call forth a common repentance and humility.

All this is only part of what we have always believed and confessed: that we live wholly by the grace and mercy of our Lord or we don't live at all. Facing walls can force us to the place where we start to live out this truth, and then things spiritual can start to happen. Until then nothing will.

Precisely at the time when we admit to the true condition of our broken-down relationships and precisely when we divorce ourselves from all phony optimism about our own powers to break through to each other, the miracle of grace occurs again and again. We discover that we are *sharing—talking—*with our high school incommunicados; we are actually being given a moment or two of insight, of understanding, of relating. We sense a new awareness of what church means and how oneness in the body of Jesus Christ and in the Holy Spirit can fling open the windows of the dank, musty cubicles that we have allowed our lives to become.

In Willa Cather's *Death Comes for the Archbishop,* on his first trip to the Southwest mission churches in his charge, Father Joseph Vaillant comes to a strange but exciting belief about miracles. He decides: "The miracles of the Church seem to me to rest not so much upon faces or voices or healing power coming suddenly near to us from afar off, but upon our perceptions being made finer, so that for a moment our eyes can see and our ears can hear what is there about us always." Our eyes and our ears do sharpen to this awareness when we receive the grace to open ourselves completely to our teen-agers, so that they see we are what we are: no more (and no less) than very human beings whose only hope and breath flow finally — if in self-interrupted current — from the mercies of God.

This is not, obviously, a comfortable stance to take in our dealings with our own children or in our leadership of youth in the church. It is never a comfortable business to confront our own weaknesses and failings, especially when we are attempting to maneuver with those over whom we have always enjoyed and still enjoy some authority. We are required now to relinquish some of our cherished position, to step down (or up) from our status as elders in our homes and churches, and to be one in Jesus Christ *with* our children. We are called, in fact, to a total reversal in form from that demanded by a code for delinquents or an academy for problem children. We are called to be servants at the same time we are masters. And we are called to see the Christ in the eyes of those we serve, by the grace and power the Creator Spirit gives us for our serving.

This does *not* mean that we ignore, or refuse to go on gathering, all the *expertise* we can in the science of adolescence and communication with adolescents. The potent developments in the psychophysical studies of teen-agers may soon reverse most of the purely chemical theories about adolescent behavior which have, to some degree, led us to an impasse in our relationships with our teen-agers. For we have come to assume that their glands, operating beyond the reach of any spiritual or other power, simply "make the kids what they are." And so we have gone also the one further, sometimes nearly fatal step of encouraging "the kids" to act out, in group form and behavior, what we have defined them to be: just blobs in chemical reaction to their endocrines, pituitaries, and mammaries. We ought not be too surprised when they follow their chemical reactions through to extremes that demand whole hospital units for young unwed mothers and courses in contraceptive devices for girls and boys in junior high schools. We are still seeing teen-agers, to a horrendous degree, through the lenses of the anatomists and biologists who, because they knew no Lord, could know only the animal and the chemical in the Lord's creations.

No one is paying a higher price for this past, now outmoded view than Christian parents and teachers in public or Christian high schools. For all of us the struggle and the waiting for the insight of *church* to dissolve the walls of glass between us and our youth are renewed every morning. And every morning the girls and boys we raise and lead and teach look at us through the self-image that our time has given them. Theirs is a world of flesh and blood and sex stimuli and expected reactions as the cost of continued belonging to "the crowd," whatever that happens to be at the time. More than anything else, it is an unreal and even grotesque world.

But there is a blessing in being one of the participants with youth when the walls crumble—if they do crumble, as they can, in the church where we give our witness. If we learn that the highest mark of being one of Christ's in the Holy Spirit is to be both *human* and *open* to our teen-agers and if we actually grow in the art of dropping, layer after layer, the defenses that have risen like walls between us, we ourselves start living to a rich and colorful depth. We drink life down to the bottom of the cup whenever we fully take part, with an adolescent girl or boy, in the sacrament of coming into the fullness of the maturity of Christ Jesus. In becoming more with them, we become more like Him. And in becoming more like Him, we become more open to all the grander possibilities of life.

During the last two years I have been corresponding

with a Sister at Our Lady of Perpetual Help High School in Brooklyn, one of those more brave souls who have taken on a ministry to the youth so violently a part of so many shallow and undersold definitions of themselves. Sister Mary reflects a constant awareness of the job she is facing, and she is most adept at describing the problems she confronts in and with "my girls," as she calls them. But there does emerge from all her letters a note of certainty and confidence that she really should have no right to claim for her ministry in an area where it is not safe to walk by night. For the glass walls are thicker in such neighborhoods than in others, and Sister Mary Francis of Assisi knows this too.

What Sister Mary has observed is that even in her New York high school the walls dissolve before a complete humanness and openness possible only to deep personal choice and dedication. Her girls do come to her with their most hidden thoughts and concerns, and in a number of ways, including the editing of a mimeographed literary magazine, she accepts their humanness into the world of her own humanness. Together they begin to achieve a consciousness of themselves as *church,* where there is no longer any need for masks or defenses. *For no one is accusing.*

Magnificent discovery! It is the essence of the church for our teen-agers. It is the pulsating breast of the home and the church they long for and fear they'll never find. And yet it is no more than, nor even as much as, the one clean sweep across the board that Paul put to paper once for all (and surely he must have been thinking of youth when he wrote it): "There is therefore no condemnation to them which are in Christ Jesus, who walk not after the flesh but after the Spirit." (Rom. 8:1)

Our church is still a healer. It is eyes to see it that we lack, and ears young enough (adolescent enough) to listen as we wait.

"I Will Have Compassion"

The girls are sitting in a comfortable half-moon circle in the hospital's front living room. There is an air of contradictory cheeriness about the flower prints in the sofa and chairs, and even the bright autumn sun streaming through a picture window looking out on acres of lawn and trees seems to be more than a little incredible.

I have been here before to lead in worship with 10 or 20 young ladies, most of them university students, and their faces betray the deepest anxiety and despair. Some of them do not bother to look up as you start the service; they do not want to reveal that much hope, for it would be a lie. They are there, some of them, out of the infinite boredom of waiting to deliver a child in a situation of utter rejection both for the child and for themselves. They are sick with grief, and there is no comfort.

Fortunately for you, as you talk with them, your own past week has had griefs of its own: sicknesses and dying in a church office that quite typically can place more stock in position than in any witness to the Lord Jesus Christ. The church is not always anything like the church, and you have felt, with others, the piercing despair of seeing and feeling her be less than she is.

So you come to them, and you open your own self also in thinking of Paul's *2 Corinthians:* "For as the sufferings of Christ abound in us, so our consolation also aboundeth by Christ." And you share the richest depth that you have — that He does come most when He seems not to come at all and that His gift of Himself is internalized in us most through the loneliness and pain and anxiety of suffering. And the girls — these teen-agers — join you that morning in the unbelievable sacrament of celebrating the presence of the Lord Jesus Christ in their drawn faces and in nerves on the verge of total rebellion.

It is an experience I will never forget, as are all experiences of those moments of complete openness with teen-agers in the midst of sufferings. And they *do* suffer! Most of us have no idea of the agonies lying behind the simplest revolts of our youth — how they wrestle through every loneliness in utter terror and apprehension. And how they long for the compassion of those who seem at once so wise and knowing and yet so harried and crushed: their adults!

Yet this is what the people of the church owe one another. And *compassion* is such a word as to frighten angels: to *suffer with,* to *participate in another's pain,* to *put self in the place of a teen-ager.* Who can do it? If we cannot recall even our own experiences of adolescence, how can we possibly become compassionate with our teen-agers now? How can we leap across a generation and put ourselves in those high school classrooms and those parked cars in the drive-ins or gaze with desperate fears at our own acned face in a bathroom mirror?

The answer is, of course, that we cannot. We can't at all, except *in* the sufferings of Jesus Christ and in our participation in those sufferings.

For this you *do* have in common with your teen-ager. You both have seen the cross and the bleeding and dying of the Savior of us all. And in the wounds of this Christ is a place where we can meet in openness and self-revealing and in that final courage which will not stop at saying:

"In my own view of Him, and in yours, we will find enough to talk about for all of life, if need be."

Alec R. Vidler, in *Christian Belief,* describes a process of life which may quite easily be viewed in the framework of adolescence.

> As at Tenebrae . . . one after another of the lights are extinguished, till one alone—and that the highest of all—is left, so it is often with the soul and her guiding stars. In our early days, these are many—parents, teachers, friends, books, authorities—but, as life goes on, one by one they fail and leave us in deepening darkness, with an increasing sense of the mystery and inexplicability of all things, till at last none but the figure of Christ stands out luminous against the prevailing night.

It is in adolescence that all the outer lights grow dim, snuff out, and finally leave us to face our final meaning—or meaninglessness—in this one uncomely Man, Jesus Christ. We confront His sufferings already in the teen years, in the new awareness of flesh and blood striving to pull us altogether out of His orbit into the orbit of self-satisfaction at whatever cost to anyone else. Make no mistake about it; this is a real pull, a persistent pull into an orbit that can last all the days of the teen-ager. Basically, it is the pull and draw of a new theology of self-gratification and finally self-worship, one that disorients the teen-ager from that total insight into self which can come through a longing view of the Christ of Golgotha.

He is, indeed, a meeting place for teen-agers and adults —if we but see in Him this meaning and this place. He crosses even those glandular bounds that separate us from our own children. His sufferings speak to them in mysterious and wonderful terms, as they speak to us after the longer heartaches of the longer years. But His sufferings speak the same language to the ears of the teen-agers as to us, and we can both hear.

And in hearing we can learn to speak again to each other.

It will be the language of humble service that we speak. It will not be the fluent language of glib answers or a language of stooping patronizingly to the needs of youth. It will be a language of mutual self-revelation and confession and mutual forgiving. It is almost the language of sacrament.

But it is the only language that the church wants to be speaking with youth. There is no time for a new psychological theory of adolescence to save our conversation or for fresh gimmicks of pop music in church to rip the Gospel away and frame it in a context "the kids can get." We are confronted by a time of estrangement and alienation, one that does indeed demand that the church be the church and that we dare to open ourselves to the infinite mercies of God by revealing ourselves to each other as what we are: eternal beggars at the throne of Christ.

But this, I suspect, is more a language than any adolescent psychology has yet outlined for us, for the fact is that Jesus Christ will Himself outlive the stilted Babels that sway alongside Him as monuments of hollowness and eternal loneliness.

We can *be* the church with our children, even in our homes, through the rite of compassion.

The Techniques of
Our Compassion

Really to help teen-agers is to suffer with them the new and threatening burdens that they are trying to carry. Since we obviously cannot do this by stepping backward into our own adolescence, we have no choice but to take the same road of quiet servanthood which our Lord Jesus Christ marked out for His own to travel.

The way, as we wrote in the last chapter, is not paved with cushions or well-lit signposts, and there are no loud-speakers to signal our direction. But there *are* certain techniques of ministering to the needs of our teen-agers, techniques that we can learn to apply in helping and healing and edifying each other in the body of Christ. If we recall them at critical times in our relationships with adolescents, we may find the doors opening to some most surprising confidences. And we may be spared some unpleasant surprises if we keep them in mind in our talking with our own high school youth.

If we are going to bear with our teen-agers, we *start by listening* very attentively to what they are trying to say about themselves. We make every conscious effort to refrain from giving any verdict on what we are hearing. We do not judge, at this point, even a thought or statement that would ordinarily outrage us. Our teen-agers have to know that we are open and self-disciplined enough to listen to them and that we respect and love them enough to listen seriously. If we cannot convince them of this, the game is lost, and there will be no further conversation — none, at least, beyond the mutual acceptance of the wall that now stands solidly between us.

We keep in mind, as we listen, that the Gospel of our Lord — and His constant and forgiving acceptance — is by no means natural or self-evident to even a deeply Christian teen-ager. The weight of guilt and regret lies so heavy in many adolescents that the Gospel has seemingly little opening into the teen-ager's experience.

Recently there arrived at my desk a letter that proves this fact even more conclusively than recent statistics demonstrating how few Christian teen-agers actually grasp their own complete forgiveness in Christ Jesus. The letter was from a 17-year-old girl who had done several remarkable articles for the youth magazine I edit and who had developed severe guilt feelings after a shattered romance with a boy not of her faith or conviction.

Bear in mind that this girl *is* a Christian and has been Christian all her life.

> This is a very hard letter for me to write, because I've never before had to go back on a promise. I can't remember a single other time in my life when I haven't been able to fulfill an obligation. But now, I'm afraid I have no choice. I'm more sorry than you can know, but I can't write the article you asked me for.
>
> It's been quite a while since you called, and ever since then I've been trying to write that article. I've written a few lines and then torn them up. They just weren't me! I couldn't understand why it should be so hard for me to write, but it was. In fact, it was impossible!
>
> It wasn't until last night, when I was lying awake in bed, that I realized what was wrong. I was lying there, trying to get some thoughts on what to write when it all of a sudden hit me. I can't write any articles on how the power of the Lord has helped me during the worst

times—simply because it hasn't! How can I write words that would help other young people when I'm in drastic need of help myself? It was a terrible realization, but it was true. God hasn't helped me to get through these last weeks since I came to Pennsylvania, because I haven't let Him. I don't even know how any more! I don't know when it got this way. Maybe it was when I left home—when I left all my family and home ties. I wasn't this way during the summer. But all of a sudden, I've found that I'm further away from God than I've ever been.

I'm up here, unable to see or talk to my mother. Don and Betty don't go to church, and I haven't been in the last 3 or 4 weeks either. I've written Will a letter that nearly broke my heart to write—telling him that it will never work between us, and when this is over I'm going to have to start all over again. (In other words, I've cut it off with him.) And now the boy that has nothing to do with all this, but whom I came to lean on this summer, and who has been writing me—helping me to keep cheerful—well, I haven't heard from him in almost a month. When I go to sleep at night, half the time I forget to pray, and when I do, it doesn't sound sincere to me. I don't know what's happened to me! I used to think I was so close to God, but maybe I never was. Maybe I was just fooling myself all along.

I'm more scared now that I've realized what is wrong than I was before. What's going to happen to me? I've always thought that no matter what happened, God had a plan for me. Was this His plan? That I should end up so far separated from Him and so afraid? I don't understand it—in fact, I don't understand anything. How could I get this way. And what's more, what am I going to do about it? I don't really know.

Anyway, I'm sorry. I've failed so many people lately, but I never thought I'd fail you or this. But I have nothing to say that would help young people. Anything I could say would only put more doubts in their minds. I don't know—maybe I've even lost the ability to write at all.

I don't know how you'll feel about this. Forgive me for breaking a promise. I tried—believe me, I tried! I'm afraid everyone overestimated me.

For this girl, as for all youth, Christian adults represent the open acceptance of the Gospel of Jesus Christ. We embody this Gospel in our own willingness to accept our young person in spite of, not because of, how or what that person communicates with us.

It is important to remember here that even loud assertions of absolute innocence betray feelings of the opposite underneath. If our teen-ager opens himself for help from us, we try to gain an insight into what is really going on beneath all the words and actions being poured out at us. And then we keep trying to develop a totally accepting attitude to this real person beneath the words. In our Christian homes, we personify for our high school youth the *forgiving authority* of God Himself.

This does not mean that we cannot voice a real view of our teen-ager's thoughts and actions—after we have done a good share of listening! We both live in a world and a time where actions have consequences. Acceptance and forgiveness do not wipe out the chain of sordid and despairing events that follow the birth of a baby out of wedlock or the "playful" theft of a car. We owe it to our youth to be down to earth and honest with him and not to coat the truth with the lies that are a peculiar temptation, it seems, for those parents gifted with the deepest faith, a faith that in the face of harsh realities may cherish false hopes.

Nevertheless, our teen-ager has to understand, *in any difficulty whatever,* that beneath *our* objective analysis of his act or thought there lies a permanent residue of forgiveness. This never changes, no matter what happens. If Christ could forgive the dying thief, we cannot withhold forgiveness and acceptance from our own teen-age child.

The pronouns of compassion are plural. When we speak with our youth, we speak always as persons caught up in the same human predicament as they. We say "we"—not "you," not "I." We do not have enough of the answers even to know what the questions are. But it is true that our teen-agers worry more about reaching through to *us* than they do about dating, and they think more about what they're going to do and who will finally be their marriage partner than they think about cars or how far to show affection or how attractive they look. The deeper you get into a teen-ager's inner life, the more close to our own sense of humanness these inner questions become, and the more closely we are, after all, able to relate to what is within.

Compassion, as it was with Jesus Christ Himself, implies a persistent willingness to suffer, and to suffer the real pain of watching helplessly while our teen-age youth suffer the equally real pain of occasional rejection by the group or physical un-attractiveness or mental and emotional distress in finding a vocation. This willingness means that we stand by, often in silence, and admit we can do nothing to help except to pray—just as we stand by in happiness at the triumphs and discoveries of our teen-ager on the school basketball team or the concert stage. It is not a morbid thing to say that this willingness to stand by, no matter what the potential cost in terms of human suffering, shapes the strongest parent and the lasting youth leader. For it is in this willingness that we most nearly approach the example of Christ Himself. And it is only the Holy Spirit who can bathe our lives with such a grace as this.

Once we possess such a grace with our children, we are on the way to demolishing the fears that, humanly speaking, do separate our own children from us. For if we are willing truly to bear each other's burdens in the Lord, and if we do not find it too terrifying to release ourselves from a rather giddy optimism that insists all high school life must be a gay success—a typically American myth—we can hardly come long under the threat of any failure as parents or homemakers or youth leaders.

"For as the sufferings of Christ abound in us, so our consolation also aboundeth by Christ." (2 Cor. 1:5)

There is indeed a ratio between our willingness to suffer with youth and our consolation in Christ Jesus. So it is completely possible that, in the words of C. S. Lewis, somewhere along the way we may even find ourselves "surprised by joy."

When We Fail

In every parent's life comes a time when he sees his own weaknesses projected back at himself in the faces of his children and when the self-accusation of *failure* is all too easily applied to himself — often for the duration of the conflict. No less common is the moment when we stand aghast at some horrendous act of desertion or rebellion on the part of someone else's teen-ager and find ourselves muttering under our breath: "And we thought *she* was such a great Christian mother!" Then accusation of *failure* flows so freely from the end of our muttered sentence or our fingertips, and our judgment is all too often as terribly final and deadly as a cleaver.

How can it happen that children from the "best" families go off and do the most impossible and unexpected things, leaving the finest parents to be embarrassed in their own profession of faith among their own friends in the church (who may tragically start to doubt the solidity of the Christian home so suddenly shattered)? What happens to reverse the current of creative living in a Christian home so shaken without apparent reason?

Even the very name of Christ seems to lie at stake when the deeply Christian family falls apart at the seams. All our glib phrases, including the repeatedly televised dictum that "The family that prays together *stays* together," collapse like cards in a windstorm, and the promises of success made by a Norman Vincent Peale start to sound like diabolically clever traps to prove us not the faithful ones after all!

Yet there we are, caught by our own or someone else's failure with our adolescents, confronted possibly by a totally ruined life in our own fellowship of faith. How do we face it all? What can we believe about it? What can we do about it?

It is right here that our faith has to become a faith of the cross more than a faith of shallow self-confidence, self-understanding, or even psychological insight into the natures of our own children. We are simply not called invariably to emerge victorious from life's assaults, and we had better know it well. Our own children will always remain mysteries either of delight or despair, and their salvation or loss may elude our strongest outreach to them.

I am reminded of W. H. Auden's lines from *For the Time Being,* in which the Mother Mary speaks to her own infant Son Christ in terms of dark wonderment:

> *Sleep. What have you learned from the womb that bore you*
> *But an anxiety your Father cannot feel?*
> *Sleep. What will the flesh that I gave do for you,*
> *Or my mother love, but tempt you from His will?*
> *Why was I chosen to teach His Son to weep?*
> *Little One, sleep.*

If there is, indeed, a single outstanding truth I have learned from 15 years of ministering to youth, parents of youth, and leaders of youth, it is that fact that all young life—even all Christian young life—hides in deepest mystery beneath all that we see of it or dare to predict about it. The Great American Sell has managed to move our high school youth into a frozen bloc of personalities well-heeled with spending money and terribly aware of every latest fad in music, cosmetics, clothes, cars, and neurotic habits. But the bloc appearance is nothing but a sham and a lie — even if we do have to cater to it at times just to get through a little to the kids who have bought the lies to preserve their own standing in the group.

Yet underneath the lie, somewhere in the shadowed caves and recesses of adolescent personality, rests the seed of God's Holy Word and Gospel trying to do its work on the core of the self. Not even the culturally sold-out teen-ager can know what's happening. And every parent sooner or later must admit his or her own helplessness at ferreting out the miracle that either is or is not going on at the center of that young heart of darkness. We are all beggars in this affair, again and again coming to that point where we prostrate ourselves before the throne of our Lord, perhaps too anxious even to form words of prayer, and finally beseeching the angels of the Lord themselves to pray for the souls of our young.

Strange comfort, isn't this? Yet who has better to offer? At the hospital where I speak on some Sunday mornings, I have met young ladies who have undergone years of psychotherapy costing to the tens of thousands of dollars, and they have not all been helped. Statistics of healing in that same hospital reveal that just as many girls recover without psychotherapy as with and that there is simply no way to predict or even hopefully to promise the wholeness of a soul, the healing of an adolescent personality.

Just as often as I face these grim statistics in confronting our failures with high school youth, I remember the stranger words of the Savior: *"Think not that I am come to send peace on earth; I came not to send peace but a sword."* And *"He that loveth son or daughter more than Me is not worthy of Me."* And then, of course, the eternal and heartrending climax: *"Take up your cross, and follow Me."*

And the cross may be the stranger in our own home.

When Christians, therefore, accuse or blame one another for failing with their children, or worse, blame *themselves* for failing, they are really blaspheming the whole depth and mystery and miracle of life in and under the Holy Spirit. Contrary to all we may long for and dream of, there are no swift and easy responses to the tragedy of blood gone wrong, and there are no Bible passages that mysticomagically will save the day of our own failure with our own youngsters. Here our faith, our theology, has to be a faith of terror and decorum before the seeming absence of God and the loneliness of the cross we find ourselves carrying, often without the least preparation on our part.

For they will not be held, these hot bloods of fresh gland and red, throbbing muscles. Part of their meaning is that they must find themselves also in breaking loose from the moorings of their faith—sometimes for only a while but sometimes for more months and years than we can stand to wait through quietly.

But isn't this perhaps the ultimate faith: to consign to our Creator and Lord and Spirit the very wholeness and salvation of our children? And then to dare simply to watch and listen (minus the pep rallies and the seemingly omnipotent Gospel hymn sing around the campfire) while our kids tell us they are not believing, why not, where they are going, and why they will *never* come back?

And then to go to our closet, close our door, and dare to say: "Even this is Yours, my Lord, I give You the results of my failure."

But it just might prove, this prayer, to be that relaxing agent to free us from an overconcern with our children—an overconcern that *can*, after all, help drive our own away from us and from the heritage of faith in our homes.

The Leaving of
a Heritage

While I was writing these chapters, the *New York Times* brought to my desk the story of Roger Allen LaPorte, a 22-year-old pacifist who set himself aflame in front of the United Nations building to protest "war, all war." It was the second such incident in a month, and it would not be the last.

The last words of the Quaker youth were, "I want to live." They were strange words, just as the action itself was a strange new tragedy to take place in a country where, theoretically at least, all protests can come forward in the form of ballots and where the voice of the people does not have to shriek or weep to be heard.

But more than anything else, the suicide revealed that the frustrations and dying hopes of youth can—even here, even with us—reach the point of no return, the point of careless sacrifice of all inheritance and *all* self and the point where society itself stands to lose all.

A political commentator ventured the guess that what caused Roger LaPorte's self-murder was the fact that the U. S. President had not as yet allowed either Senate or populace to vote for or against the expansion of the war in Vietnam. There may have been some truth to the observation, but the remark may also prove too narrow a definition of the vast feeling of helplessness among our teen-agers and even our Christian youth. I believe we have far too limited an understanding of this hollow sense of helplessness—this sense that a world of cruel and cold complexity is maneuvering and manipulating their lives without any chance of a retort powerful enough to do any good or any effective changing.

It is this desperation, this carelessness, that brands our high school youth as "strangers in the house," as one Roman Catholic priest termed them. And the carelessness is so much the more puzzling and threatening to Christian parents and youth leaders because it emerges from an anxiety too vague to identify and lashes out at objects of love which have not the least thing in common with the anxiety breeding the terror. No one escapes the new fury of campus youth flaring into riots; the finest college presidents suffer defeat along with the worst, simply because anxiety and mob charges can't tell the difference between fine and bad college presidents.

Even the church is not spared this defeat. Roger Allen LaPorte was a Quaker, and his church does not sanction protest suicides. It is entirely probable that Protestant churches of all stripes are going to feel the brunt of the sacrifice of religious heritage, and the protest of terror beyond all rational control, as the complexity and seeming injustice of our kind of country in our kind of world increases. I can see no way out of this for us.

For the truth is that what *was* once a more or less vulnerable social structure—vulnerable at least to the attacks of a Henry Ford or a Thomas Edison or a George Washington Carver—has in the years since World War II quite obviously outraced the abilities of *leaders* of men to comprehend all the factors involved. It was inwardly devastating for most of us to learn that even President John F. Kennedy's brave decision to confront Russia over the Cuban missile installations was prefaced (as we discovered later) not only by the diaried revelations of a top Russian deserter but by incredibly detailed and voluminous computer analysis. And what if the computer had said, indeed, that Russia had one more ICBM in place and aimed than we? What if the scientist deserter had not revealed that Russia's main arsenal, her only arsenal in actual battle readiness, was her IRBM batteries of Europe?

The grim truth is that such complexity does not leave room for much personal creative thought or personal creative action. It leaves room only for mass drafting of infantry, mass deployment of atomic warheads, massed headlines in the single human being of depth and vision.

Amid all the helpless frustration and bitterness a young spirit feels in the face of this mass machinery (and all it implies about what life *seems* to be), the values and promises of any religious heritage are only lost computer tape. To the impatient adolescent, the church itself often appears to be standing wall-like with the machines, the computers, the 40-story office buildings, and the white-coated technicians. There is the feeling, *who can win through all this if even a Kennedy based what we thought was bravery on the spinning numbers of an IBM?* There is the implied — if not often spoken — question, *What does it matter, this doctrine or that, this faith or that, when finally the numbers will give the verdict on God, just as the numbers gave the verdict on Cuba and Khrushchev's demise and the draft card I have to carry?*

Too often, we have to admit, the church does join the game on the side of the computer and starts to treat her people as figures without names, as contributors to an organization deserving to be kept alive for its own sake rather than for the sake of the persons who supposedly *are* the church. I have been in cathedrals where from one year to the next there was no pastor at the door even to try to meet the shadows who dart into the pews, pray silently and perhaps desperately, and then hurry out

61

again into the Lord knows what night and loneliness in the crowd.

It is safe for the church to be there—on the side of the technicians and the machines—if only for the fact that much of her membership have hands on the buttons of the machines. The great Upper Middle Class runs the action, or thinks it runs the action, in both computer room and narthex. The youth don't run anything—and they know it. And they sense with a bitterness approaching desertion that the fingers on the light switches in the narthex cloakroom are the same that control the automation buttons.

From here it is only a small and simple step to a religion of *both* society and church that makes of membership rolls only more rubber stamps. Among our thoughtful youth today, this equation adds up to an inner argument so powerful that it can compel even the leaving of *all* heritage. It can compel that utter loneliness of cutting off all one's roots in one final and absolute, and terribly foolhardy, effort to get free of society by not admitting what has already become a fact: *There are instances in which I am only a number, but I am determined to keep them as few in number as possible.*

Roger Allen LaPorte was not willing to accept the conditional life with numbers. He could not absorb into himself, say, the possibility that in the next election his vote—*against* the President who, in his opinion, had needlessly escalated the war in Vietnam—might be overwhelmed by 2 million other votes *for* this President. For the young man, therefore, only a completely outrageous protest would do: a protest that would make the front page of every newspaper in this country and at least several others. The protest was made, the stories were run, the President said nothing, and the war in Vietnam went on while the computers deep in the bowels of the Pentagon clattered happily along. They didn't even smell the gasoline, much less record the burning of a young man.

But see the things all this says about young life now, even about what it is to go to high school and confront one's first computerlike analysis of the birth of the world — in eons, not thousands of years. See how simple it can be for an adolescent to make the crucial inner decision that *he really does not matter in all this*. Let us be sure that the decision is being made every day in thousands of even Christian homes, by young and still-tender minds whose faith is simply overwhelmed by the enormous weights and balances of a century gone half-mad on space exploration, guerilla warfare, and armed service training. It is no accident that the best-selling magazine among teenagers bears the one-word epitaph *MAD*.

So the heritage of faith can be left out of the frustration and loneliness in young girls and boys moving into a world they never made, but one made indeed of the small white number-wheels we all, I think, instinctively hate. If, in spite of all this, the church could only be that last place and being on earth where we could rediscover our souls, our own true selves, by knowing ourselves as accepted and loved and lighted by all the throne of our Lord Jesus Christ!

Is it so impossible for us to be this, if only to keep the heritage of this same Jesus Christ in living trust for our own flesh and blood?

A Teen-Age Hope for Oneness

Almighty God, give us grace that we may cast away the works of darkness, and put upon us the armour of light, now in the time of this mortal life, in which Thy Son Jesus Christ came to visit us in great humility.

This collect of the church for the First Sunday in Advent does not lie far from the inner longings of a youth who has found in his own heritage of faith not quite enough to sustain him and so has left it all for some imaginary field of faith. The same youth may talk wistfully of the Man Jesus Christ, yet without commitment to Him, something like an old and warped phonograph record being played over and over again without meaning. There is a sense of drift and guilt and nameless foreboding and lack of certainty of any kind. There is a sense of darkness. And there is a sense of being torn apart between past and future, between old myths and new lies, and of being betrayed by both.

Adolescence is like this, a shattering of the mirror that once held such a crystal-clear image of self and home and church and life. And now light itself gleams afar off like an armour, out of reach but still to be prayed for. Old faith seems impossible, and new faith ridiculous, and both utterly desirable and unattainable.

The church itself comes to symbolize the shattering of the adolescent's inner mirror. Each denominational assertion of infallibility, each imprecation of one Christian upon another, adds to the shattering and the confusion. For the adolescent realizes all too sharply how many churches lay claim to the truth, lay hands on the Gospel and swear possession, and what is he to think or imagine? Who is right? Who is wrong? Or is right or wrong itself a bit of tattered rag drifting amid the odd pieces of glass that were once a whole mirror?

Precisely here is where the scandal of apartness in the churches moves into persons to become the cancer of spiritual confusion and dying. When the adolescent starts to identify his own inner emotional jigsaw puzzle with the perplexity of rival churches claiming at once universal love *and* universal truth, in the competing appeals and conflicting claims he may find arguments for outright rejection of the church and, by acting accordingly, may forfeit his greatest hope of maturing beyond personal shatteredness: at the same time he confirms himself in loss of commitment to the throne of Jesus Christ.

The identification is diabolical but emotionally beyond the reach of most adults. So often the identification takes place in the last year of high school or the first in college and hangs over for a lifetime in some suburbia of defeat and doubt. And most churches blithely barge on in complete unawareness of the internalization of their scandal of apartness — the personalization of it in the faces and eyes of those young people who suddenly look at their denomination as if they have never known her and will never profess to know her again.

This is a hard fact for me to write about; like most adults, I grew up in a denomination, and to mine I owe even my education and my profession. I could not wish to seem ungrateful for all my denomination has truly meant to my own growth as a person with the gift of faith from my Lord and Savior Jesus Christ. Yet even in the protected walls of a high school seminary I was confronted with the perplexing lovelessness of a single teacher who railed at my own synod from the truth-possessed confines of his, and the identification of this obvious confusion soon became one with my own inner state. There was no avoiding the grand and final question so well put by Pontius Pilate: "What *is* truth?"

No adult heard my question, for I feared that the mere asking of it would brand me as one to be watched in the seminary. Yet I suspect that my classmates asked it too, in many forms and ways, and some perhaps left the ministry itself because their own inner shattered mirrors could find no balancing wholeness in a church that was one and serene in her Lord and her Holy Spirit.

What a thing such a church might have been to us then! For the first time I came to understand why the last prayer of Jesus Christ was a prayer "that they may be one, as You and I, Father, are one!" He, the Christ, must have foreseen what shapes and myriad forms this church of His would take in its wars of the future. And He must have known what wounds almost beyond healing this separation would leave on especially the young souls growing into the church with all the hopes and prayers possible only to teen-age romantics on their lips. And He must have seen even how this shatteredness of the church could add to the normal shatteredness of new gland secretions and stranger self-doubts during the torturous emergence into adult life. A teen-ager may well know more than we imagine why Jesus Christ prayed the way He prayed!

But this *is* the way the church has come to us and is and must be for us now. We all pray that the church may become one in truth, in the truth of the Holy Spirit. *But how do we tell our youth now, in the heat of the day, that the con-*

fusion must stand? How do we say we have no present answer to the division of the church, even though we understand that this division can become internalized in the personalities of our own youth?

There are several ways, I believe, in which we can help our Christian adolescents meet this inner *and* outer dilemma. They take some courage and some doing, and in some cases they demand that we even take a stand against what may mistakenly have been taught by one denomination or another.

The first way: We can say that the division of the church is only a present fact of history and certainly not by any means a hope. For even in our divided state we continue to long for that one communion for which our Lord prayed to His Father just before His ultimate sacrifice. In our homes we reflect this longing by talking of that day when the church may in fact *be* one, and in our communication with our neighbors of other faiths we give our hope substance by our will to love even those to whom dividedness has become a way of life.

The second way: We can make the hope of one church a continuing theme of our family and group and private prayers. A prayer is not an unreal mystique to an adolescent aware of this inner longing for oneness, for making whole the shattered mirror. More likely a prayer takes on the form of a sacrament of internal growing and maturing toward the nature of the Christ. Since at this stage even the pulpit and the altar can be confused, in the teen-ager's mind, with the divided church, a prayer life of depth presents the realities of things unseen and hopes yet unborn. The one church of all believers, now invisible, crystallizes in the liturgies of collects and in the unspoken words of adolescent psalms and hymns and spiritual songs.

The third way: We can represent in our own selves, which have been touched by the accepting love and courage of Jesus

Christ, the unity and integrity of that one church that will some-day—by the Holy Spirit—come into the fullness of time. And this is the thorniest road of all, of course, for the very divisions and separations that our teen-agers internalize have left their marks also on us. The marks show whether we much like them to or not, often just *when* the perplexities that have scarred us come to the surface in our dealings with youth.

But in all reality the unity of the church must become symbolized in Christian parents and pastors and teachers and youth leaders, or that unity can mean little in the joining of church bodies and the writing of new confessions. The church today remains an offense to teen-agers in a state of disorientation and perplexity; the Christ cannot stay divided, and the Holy Spirit will see to that. But meanwhile we must *be* the church to our youth, the guarantors to them of the one church that is surely to be, even if we can testify now only to its invisible shadow of the future.

There is one more way: We can work toward this oneness by simply accepting nothing less as our future promise and by calling on our high school youth to play out their role in meeting this promise. They are probably more adept at doing just this than we can possibly dream at the present, and I can only venture a well-cultivated guess that our churches are already moving swifter than we imagine.

The winds of the Spirit blow full and free to our day, and heighten with the threats and counterthreats of an era speckled with the dust of hydrogen bombs and the debris of lost space vehicles. The last space vehicle may be circling our planet long after we have gone—long after all men have gone.

But never doubt that the Holy and Creator Spirit will have had His say. And never question that our Christian teen-agers will carry a large part of His message with them.

Tell Us:
We Are Never Alone

Youth wants and prays for the oneness of the church in the hope that somehow this unity can transcend the separatedness and the apartness of adolescence. But even beyond this, there is in the teen-ager a constant need for that fellowship and support which only a complete theology of the whole church in history can offer.

I am speaking of that long thin line of saints and martyrs, pastors and angelic hosts, who have in past times served as models of spiritual growth and power to the new lights of the church. I am thinking of those hymns that only teen-agers can sing with some instinctive understanding and insight: "For All the Saints Who from Their Labors Rest," and "The Son of God Goes Forth to War," and all those mighty songs of glory for the long thin line of sunlight leading down to the present church of youth and some uncertainty. And I am not forgetting those post-sacramental remembrances also of the apostles—and even the Mother Mary—which also continue that sense of historical continuity and fellowship which adult worshipers, in their concern with the statistical present, are all too prone to forget.

Our Protestant churches have not quite come to see how desperately young Christians need a theology of the church that crosses the fading line of time and moves with the hosts of eternity. That *Weltschmerz* that is so often the butt of jokes about teen-agers is often nothing more or less than an intense longing for this eternal dimension in the church, in the parish homes, and in the youth group where the church is to be realistically and concretely defined and played out in the teen-age context.

It is not hard to understand why Protestants have thinned down their theology of the church, sometimes to a series of fundamental statements for acceptance by the faithful, sometimes to even less — a mere signing of a white membership card of *Intent to Participate,* or something of that order. But we ought to know that the easier and the more absurdly simple we make membership in our churches, the less likely our youth are going to be to buy that membership. They do not want to feel that they are joining a club with skin-deep demands on them.

The fact is that they want a church that will quietly ask for a total commitment to all that the church has ever been and ever will be: to the Lord of the church, Jesus Christ, Gift of the Father by the power of the Holy Spirit; and to the endless song of the martyrs and the saints who have gone on before, all self-giving for the sake of that church of Jesus Christ.

Obviously, this theology of the long thin line of the church shatters also that diabolical view of death which has been foisted on our teen-agers and ourselves by the immensely clever technicians of death, the undertaking parlors and the deceiving sham of cosmeticians and embalmers who, in trying to give the *illusion* of life at the wrong time, actually convey instead the fear of the *permanence* of death. No one is more a victim of this trickery than our adolescents, whose innermost terror before the first signs of death in themselves cries out for the church to preach again and again that high reality of the throne of the Church Victorious, where already now the song is being raised to the Lamb by the souls who have never died.

To see all of life as part of this divine continuity—from the right hand of God through the saints in glory to the succession of the faithful in the church even now—cannot help but stabilize and balance the tremendous inner charges and retreats of adolescents. Eternal life may seem a vague and faraway theological dream, but not to a youngster on a sickbed or to those who have learned to live in its glowing dimension with a teen-age Sunday morning group. I have seen this theology of the Church Eternal change and revive a group of gradually disappearing Christian teen-agers, and I have noticed more than once that church youth programs that manage to hold onto their youth are often intensely aware of the dimension of eternal life.

If only for the sake of our teen-agers, then, we would do well to reexamine our motives for thinning down our theology of the church as we have and for shutting out that dim but heroic light the church in glory can shine on the frantic times of youth. Under what mistaken notions of post-Reformation altar and symbol smashers have we allowed also the historic meaning of the heroes of faith to be diminished for our church's youth? By what fear of idolatry have we also cut ourselves—and our high school Christians—off from every root except, perhaps, the heroes of the Reformation itself?

We must remain concerned about this simply *because heroes* are *so vital to adolescents, and a concept of life beyond reach of death does really touch on almost every present predicament of youth.* For which single question of a teen-ager, from the parked car to the choosing of a career, does not fall into perspective when viewed in the light of eternity? We do not want to miss out on that perspective which only the lives and deaths of those who have gone on before can lend to our own lives amid daily threats of dying.

For years one of my favorite books has been *A Time of Gods*, a volume of photos by Roloff Beny on the text of Homer's *Odyssey*, composed of almost marblelike pictures of the Greek statues and scenes that later surrounded a teen-age girl or boy growing up in the days of Paul the apostle. We do not have to marvel too much at the magnificent spirits produced in such surroundings, for the culture in which youth matures helps more than we think to mold—and possibly even to create—that greatness of soul so rare in lives unblessed with the gigantic shadows of the past.

It is quite possible, in the miracle of adolescence, for the gigantic shadows of the past to become those models, those friends, that serve to dispel (or at least decrease) both the loneliness and the terribly overhanging weights of death and uncertainty. For in the Christian realm of things, nothing is *more* certain than our endless unity in praise around the throne of Jesus Christ, the taking of our place with the saints and the martys around that throne, and the fact that even now the smallest events of our days are guided and governed by that throne.

Nothing is more certain than this: *We are never alone.* And we cannot help but want to say this, in as many ways as we can possibly say it, to the teen-agers in our care.

Around the aloneness and the perplexity of their experiences—which we can never really reach into—we *can* wrap the warm fellowship of the church of eternity, the Church Victorious, the church of the heroes. We *can* keep recalling for our teen-age youth the fact of the deathlessness of the soul and the certain resurrection of the body and the victory of the Lord of life and death even over the deceitful funeral arrangements to which we (for now, at least) give a place in our church rites. Perhaps right here, in fact, is the moment when we can say the most with the fewest words. For perhaps even the cosmetician's makeup betrays an infinite human longing to believe exactly that which the deep Christian faith offers to those who will move into it: life without end, under the throne of the King of kings, who is not without His chorus of praise and glory and relentless joy.

Someday, perhaps, all of us in the church will see that even the earthy problems of youth are basically theological problems. And we will see that the *only* final answers to adolescence are the answers that faith whispers to the young human spirit. All this may put a few of the semi-psychological, semijournalistic columnists out of business. All of this may also help to put the church of Jesus Christ back in business as far as teen-agers are concerned.

The Risk unto Life:
Youth Leading the Church

Most of us have grown up in churches where the first qualification for leadership is a God-given bonus of gray hair and a clear, if aged, eye looking paternally down upon youth. In my own church, no young man of 46 could have aspired to the rank of denominational president — even in the year when a 46-year-old upstart named John F. Kennedy swept into the White House to lead the most powerful nation of the world.

It is characteristic of such churches and such leadership that little or no consideration is given to the effect of this policy on really gifted young leaders — boys *and* girls — who in their teens are casting an eye about to discover areas where they can invest their energies and their talents of leadership. We find it possible even to conduct surveys to determine why seminary enrollments are falling off and going by default too often to second-rate students — without once looking thoroughly at our own policies of church leadership.

Which young man worth his salt would join a firm where the prime prerequisite for advancement to leadership is a mane of gray? Such corporations quickly go begging for leadership, and soon lose the game to outfits with the courage to promote a McNamara to the chair of leadership.

Granted that the church is no Ford Motor Company, it *is* a human organization heavily dependent on the human qualities of leadership and creativity now already residing in its youth. To frustrate and in fact to wall off these gifts of the holy Creator Spirit by consciously or unconsciously adopting a philosophy of aged leadership is to mortgage the future of the church by discounting its most precious resources.

It is exactly this philosophy of leadership that leads the best-endowed teen-agers not even to take seriously the calls of their church—the pamphlets and the campaigns to fill the posts of service and the challenges to lives of sacrifice in the mission fields. Service and sacrifice are not beyond the longings of youth, but neither is responsibility. And it may be quite significant that Christ's own apostles, given the overwhelming responsibility to lead the young church through its crucial early days, were not at all in the age of gray hair but closer to the years of a Kennedy.

Amid the never-ceasing drain for war service and with the accelerating development of new and skilled technologies, the calls for sensitive and trainable youth are not going to taper off but will increase to a degree we now dismiss as incredible. Our churches are yet going to see days when seminaries will be half filled, a third of the pulpits vacant, and posts of creative service staffed by largely unequipped personnel trying to carry double loads of work. And if the leadership incentive of the church remains nil for youth capable of future leadership, the critical problem of filling the outposts of the church will treble in intensity. The signs of this situation are already with us, and the signs are written unusually large in the brightest eyes among our adolescent boys and girls.

Each Sunday morning my own razor-sharp group of teen-agers hint about their deeply held attitudes toward service in the church, and sometimes the hints cause me to pray long and hard for a church that is going to need a few of these blessings. One of the boys, endowed with an I. Q. close to 140, a natural leader from a home rich in service to the church, has already rejected any possibility of the holy ministry. He senses, by the way he speaks at least, that the ministry would soon frustrate any leadership initiatives by the sheer woolen weight of rigidity and seniority patterns in even the congregational sphere. Another in the group, a girl who would make a brilliant contribution to the church as a teacher, has already accepted a scholarship offer from a college that will in all likelihood lead her not only into a vocation radically disconnected from church and church teaching but also away from any real self-giving in an area at all connected with her finest gifts.

But the worst is that our Sunday discussions of the needs of the church cannot break down and dispel the suspicion that professional service in the church is somehow a surrender of talent and initiative, that the church actually does not *want* uncompromised commitment and goals of leadership, and that only the medical or space-age professions have room for utter self-commitment and total self-fulfillment. It is a bitter Sunday morning for me to think that young spirits given the benediction of the Lord's highest natural blessings may pour most or all of these gifts into the crucible of war machinery, mainly out of fear that the church of Jesus Christ has grown too old to accept and risk the leadership of the young.

Yet that is, from where I view it, the truth about the future of the holy Christian church and its crisis of leadership and creative service. And I see no immediate change possible in the policies that have helped to produce this coming crisis, whose first edges are already with us.

For the equally distressing truth is that our necessity

to make age itself a first qualification for leadership on almost any level of church life stems not from any rational or spiritual springs but rather from an innate and intense fear that the freedom and adventurous commitment of youth might plunge *us* into a commitment beyond the sage and familiar outlines of our past white picket fences. Such a possibility strikes us as dangerous and threatening to our complacency and even our security, especially if we happen to occupy some of those offices more or less responsible for our church life at present.

But in all this we may fail to ask the most crucial question of all, the question that has caused theologians of scope and insight to predict the downhill skid of our Christian churches. *What if our safe fences no longer appeal to a younger generation to whom the very idea of mere safety seems quaintly out of date in an age when any actual safety will never be experienced by any of us again?* How will the church live without the lifeblood of these risky teen-agers and their wild dreams of utter and total commitment?

Now we see more clearly the alternatives. We either risk the church unto death in the continuing of our premium on age, or we risk the church unto life by daring to believe that the Holy Spirit can hold within *true* safety the visions and outpoured energies of youth. In any case, we have to go with the best we have, or we cannot call ourselves faithful even to the Power and Life who by the Gospel of Jesus Christ has taken over the personalities and wills of this strange new crowd within our churches.

Perhaps the final question might be why we have allowed safety itself to come to matter so much to us — so much that we would stake our souls on its priority. Is any denomination so precious that its temporal security outranks the free spirits of its own young souls? Can any of us claim to have delineated finally and for all the safety lines of the Spirit? To whose even-so-wise leadership would we entrust that which only the Holy Spirit Himself can guarantee?

It is true that to commit our treasures to the futures of our teen-agers is a risk. It is true that to confront our teen-agers now with the full confessions of our own commitments—and the husks of our failures—is a risk. Sometimes the risk is so great that we can never on our own find courage to venture it.

But what is the alternative to the risk with our youth? Isn't the alternative, finally, the death of our churches as effective though human organizations? Or how will we survive without the finest and most spirited young leaders our Lord has given us?

And how will our young survive without a church to watch when they begin to stand, listen when they begin to speak, and follow when they begin to lead?

The Size of
a Teen-Age Life

The whole of our Christian faith and hope in eternal life has an immense meaning for youth and those responsible for guiding youth. As the line of demarcation between time and the kingdom of heaven diminishes and as the draw of the purely secular — the popularity, the position, the money, the entertainments, the cars, the ranch-type home — fades in power, a new dimension comes into being and takes over the personality.

It is the dimension of the eternally ongoing life that emerges now: the life that does *not* end, ever. The person who does *not* really die, ever. The teen-ager who will *not* simply grow old and outlive human usefulness, ever. For in the kingdom of heaven that teen-ager's soul (as our own) lives on in endless prayer and praise with the chorus of the angels and the saints and martyrs, and there is no end to the joy and the singing, the infinite pageant of mystery and meaning encircling the throne of the Lamb of God.

That we have not always drawn on this pageant for our evaluation of our own youth and our approach to them and our patience with them — and with ourselves when we miss them — is understandable only in the light of our dim vision of what this kingdom of heaven really is like and what it does to the human life it enters and transforms.

We are worse off here than someone trying to project teen-age life onto a screen through a projector with one lens missing. The image always gets shattered on the way.

So it is no surprise that Christians, too, suffer under the strain of a constant effort to see more clearly the dimensions of their own lives in the changing spectrum of light cast from the throne. This is, to me, the major reason for the depressions, the lassitude, the weariness that perpetually astound us when we, teen-agers or adults, start to think that our faith is at its strongest. For precisely at that point we feel most intensely the strain of trying to see the fullest possible dimensions of life under the Kingdom.

I am not saying that the strain is misspent effort or bound to such ultimate frustration that we had best not strain at all to see. We owe it to our youth to make the perpetual effort, painful as it may be, to view them even as those eternal souls they cannot yet discern themselves to be. For in our eyes they may soon come to see themselves anew, and our own faces may provide exactly the mirror they need to grow into the Kingdom.

Although they see through a glass darkly, as all of us must, our teen-agers are not blind to the possible dimensions of their souls, their personalities. More than at any other age, they are ready in fact to confront this dimension in all its implications for their present, past, and future. And they will venerate the parent or youth leader who can mirror this eternal dimension of the young soul in his very attitude and approach to them: in the way he looks at them and listens to them and talks with them.

This does not cancel out humor, light speech, and the occasional use of teen-age jargon, or an idiom close to jargon, to reach through to teen-agers. Quite the opposite, in fact. For if we start to realize that our *inner* evaluations of young souls will say more to these souls than words, or even sermons of words, we will become more free to let loose and drop our need to overwhelm, impress, sermonize, or convince by sheer weight of argument. This simply doesn't work anyway, as we well know, and only arouses our young persons to raise higher the wall that separates us.

It is a strange and delightful thing that the more we come to see the eternal dimensions of the soul, the teen-age personality, and the size of that young life, the more contemporary, the more at ease, and the more human in every sense we can afford to be with youth. In this light a Puritan, overserious, or even moralistic approach to teen-age youth reveals in the parent or teacher not a vibrant faith but a faith that has not yet quite come to see even partially the dimensions of deathlessness in Jesus Christ, in the stream of which our sons and daughters actually can thrive and grow. One cannot help but wonder at the tragic perversion by which the church of Jesus Christ and the Holy and Creator Spirit has come to be identified *with* Puritan moralism and legalism, especially in the area of parenthood and youth work. Granted that prudence dictates a certain amount of ethical standard-bearing in our dealing with our teen-agers, there is really no excuse for confusing these standards with the kingdom of heaven and all it implies for us and our young Christians.

The young soul that, redeemed and blessed, will never die; the stream of grace flooding into that soul on the light beams of heaven itself; and the healing grace we have already received and carry about in us as quiet testimony to the reality of the blessed Christ and all around Him—all this provides us a youth-faith utterly dynamic for this age of sharp endings in which we live and work. We are handling here a power that radiates out far beyond ourselves or our poor contrivances. We are wielding the force, the final reaches of the force, of the Gospel of

Jesus Christ. And that Gospel remains incredibly potent to change young human life, young human personality, young visions of what it means to be a king and a priest in the household of our Lord Himself. That Gospel of Jesus Christ moves and changes beyond the fences of educational techniques or psychology, beyond even the admitted miracles of transformation possible in psychotherapy. That Gospel is something all its own, and it is ours.

There are all kinds of reasons to believe that even the church today has lost its pristine evaluation of this Gospel: this total vision of its power in and over human life. Not the least of these reasons is the evidence, obvious almost everywhere, that the churches talk more of buildings and budgets than they do of persons. It is as if the buildings were eternal and the persons short-lived, as if we were all here to erect and serve new buildings. Meanwhile, nothing remains more difficult than to acquire financing, either in congregations or in denominational headquarters, for more consistent and more helpful approaches to young persons. Teen-agers especially are viewed as the most transient of beings, whose value—as far as the churches are concerned—is questionable and dubious. To many who have worked in youth leadership under these circumstances, it is a day-by-day wonder that teen-age youth stay with the church as loyally as they do. For the low opinion of high school youth is most obvious to those who suffer most from it—the young girls and the young boys—and the foundation of the low opinion is equally obvious: the lack of spiritual insight into the size of a teen-age soul and the duration of a teen-age life.

The recovery of our spiritual vision will not be easy, and it will not be swift. Too long we have allowed the shallowness of purely chemical and biological views of man to smother our sense of miracle when we confront a child.

Too unconsciously have we whittled away at the visions of the eternal Kingdom so amply supplied by the Revelation of St. John and even by the poems of Dante and Milton and the brilliantly instinctive and suffusing theology of all of Shakespeare. But the truth is that we will either recapture this spiritual vision in all its impact or personality, or we will continue as churches on a downhill slide toward the same empty, indeed nihilistic, views of both eternity *and* personality that we once associated with blind unbelief.

All of Christian youth work, and writing on youth, and youth counseling, is deeply theological, deeply spiritual. For in the deepest and most intense Christian sense, the queer science of theology must overwhelm and take captive even those Freudian insights and discoveries that have revolutionized our current views of what it is to be human. If we are not willing to suffer through to the redemption of these views by purely Christian analysis, we hardly deserve the honor of leading young people in peculiarly Christian worship or study. We could best leave youth and all their study to the social technicians or to the educational technicians—without benefit of faith or hope.

As I see it, the choice lies quite challengingly before the churches right now, and a lot of social and educational technicians are daring the churches to do anything at all about it. For obviously, those who see no eternal dimension to the soul, the person, are not inclined to admit that anyone else *really* does either. To the manipulators of society, from the atheistic bureaucrat to the atheistic schoolteacher around the corner, the Christian claim to life relevance sounds not only ridiculous but hypocritical.

And perhaps to our teen-agers this opinion is beginning to make sense. For apparently the churches are not following through on what they claim to believe (if they claim to believe much of anything anymore), and the social manipulators seem to be carrying the day. And even if they are not, even if the full relevance and power of the Gospel of Jesus Christ may be asserted by the churches in the future, many young souls may be lost in the wait.

But that is a prospect we do not want to succumb to even for a moment.

The Young Church
Is *for Us*

There is a great deal of resentment among parents and leaders of teen-agers over their obvious and sometimes obviously insolent rejection of the adult world: its values, its virtue of industry and reward for industry, its compromises of the organization, the shady deal, and the slick salesmanship of the TV commercial and the car salesman.

This rejection occasionally reaches the pitch of revolt and even dares to move within the settled walls of the churches, where it is not only most unexpected but also most unwelcome. At this Christian adults rise up in horror and often do not hesitate to identify the revolt as anti-Christ, antichurch, anti everything worth holding by adults who know what life is all about. We find it too easy to dispel the whole wretched business with the indignant question: *What in the world is going to happen to the church when these kids get hold of it?* (As if they don't have "hold of it" already!)

It's a fine question, but quite preliminary. We have not yet looked deeply enough into what our teen-agers are trying so deviously, and so painfully, to say to us. They are *not, they* know, trying to reject us and our attempt to live in a world we never made. What they *are* trying to do, often in their own piteously frantic way, is to alert us to the falseness of our own ways, the self-deceptions of our own conceits, the half-measuredness of our own faith.

85

They are trying to say as well as they can: *Please, for the sake of our souls, examine again the world of values you want us to buy from you. Are you sure this is the heritage you want to pass on to us?*

It is, we must admit, a fair question—even from teen-age youth, who may not always know how to ask it, much less how to answer it. For all they sense, most of them, is a vague discomfort at an equally vague "phoniness" in us. We do not seem to be holding together. The way we live so often violates what we say we believe, and what we affirm so often makes the way we live appear devastatingly small and insignificant.

It is not an accusation easy to take or light to carry. For the situations and operations of the adult world *do* force us into compromises that violate our own Christian conscience. After 15 years of editing in the church, I am aware that such violations of conscience occur even where, theoretically, the Gospel of Jesus Christ should in all expectation prohibit them. But we do not live in an obliging world, and even our closest friends may at times lead us into compromises that we know are not in agreement with our faith but which we make simply to keep on living. It is often, in fact most often, a gray and muddy world—and we slosh about in it more uneasily as we come to see more and more clearly what we need to be as Christians in such a world.

Our teen-agers do not ease this uneasiness. With their constant queries and the question marks written boldly on their faces, they remind us of all our compromises of conscience and *self,* and they keep prodding us to live out our open and honest commitment to the kingdom of heaven. Should they spare us the unsettling reproach implied by their questions, they may quietly threaten to buy the compromises, the cheap and phony values, that we may not profess but do actually live by. And the latter is by far the worse condemnation!

And as usual we are tempted to trace to arrogance or even disobedience the pain and unease their confrontation brings us. It is not pleasant to feel aggravated by one's own children, and when we do, we tend as well to blame *them* as to look at ourselves. Suddenly they seem enemies in our homes, disgruntled young persons with beatnik tendencies, ungrateful to their parents and disruptive of their parents' values. And, to put it frankly, teen-agers are most gifted at pulling off this act—especially once they sense we are casting them in the role of arrogant ones.

But even then, perhaps in spite of themselves, our youth are not as unconscious of *our* needs as we may suppose. Inwardly they remain most aware that the adults around them are fighting some sort of a battle which is not always, by a long shot, going in one direction. Nor is the victory certain. Long before his or her coming of age, the teen-ager senses that the adult world is vicious beyond the imagining of youth and that in this world it is anything but easy to *act* as a Christian.

So the teen-ager's call to us is not altogether self-centered. And the youth who form the young church of our time are not really a far-out, unaware, cynical group interested only in jazz liturgies and folk singers. Far from it, they are more sensitive to the implications of their Christian confession than is good for our comfort. They love us with a love that is more honest than we can stand, and they express their love in terms that gnaw and bother us. I have had a teen-ager tell me after a sermon, "But can you *live* the way you said?" And the remark was made in a fiercely honest kindness. I, as you, have experienced in my home the blistering honesty of a teen-ager's comment on some betrayal of myself in company or in public. Again, there was the call back to self and Christ's Spirit in self and to all that I had learned to desert so glibly and so smoothly for that time.

Our teen-agers, contrary to what we may imagine, are

more than aware that this desertion, so wholesale among Christian adults, will not work in the long run. In trying to call us back to rigorous honesty, freedom from phoniness, and the reality of Christian commitment, they are trying in the only way they know to save the souls of their parents and leaders. For they may realize better than we that to play the games we are required to play in our adult world is indeed to risk one's own soul.

And in this act of reaching out to us, our youth take *their* place in the long thin line of witnesses and saints and angels who have streamed into the lives of countless petitioners of Christ, Lord of heaven and earth, for aid in the conflicts of life. Our most serious mistake would be to underestimate their power, for our youth also bear in themselves the indwelling holy Creator Spirit, and in their call to us—painfully as that call may come—they voice once more the ageless concern of the Gospel "that ye serve not idols, but the living God."

And I sometimes wonder whether it is altogether distrust of youth that leads us to despise teen-agers so readily, or whether it is not in fact a certain fear of their honesty— and their commitment—that sets us up as a wall against them. In the church at least, teen-agers are not quite the tyrants we say they are, and this we know quite well. Nevertheless our resentments are numerous, and we coddle them at all cost, if only for a defense!

But this, too, is done at the cost of a church that might, if given half a chance, bridge the gap between adolescent and adult and wipe out all that *is* commercial and phony in the area we label *teen-age*. The teen-age church may be, ultimately, on our side, but we would rather keep it where it was, safely out of sight, carefully penned up in the fences of some integrity and honesty that might pain us beyond even the present.

So again, it is possible for us to disrupt the succession

of grace which the Lord of the church has given us. And by giving our own youth short shrift we again divide what should never be divided: the body of Jesus Christ, the seamless robe of our Lord. The young church remains the young church, and we the old, and never the twain shall meet — at least not if we have anything to say or do about it!

The trouble is that we do: we have too much to say about it. For we too stand in the line of grace streaming from the kingdom of heaven, and our teen-agers must wait for us to transmit to them the day-by-day newness of the love of the King of kings.

They have nowhere else to go.

Toward Power
in Their World

Even a mature church, a global church if you will, dare never exist for itself alone. And so this young church, this young tree growing in the grove of trees we call the adult church, must sooner or later let the winds of the Holy Spirit carry its seed wheresoever the Spirit wills. And the Spirit wills to move into the world, always with a power and purity that upset the nice balances of conformity and secular ritual.

This is why the church in our own time has suddenly become involved in all sorts of activities which deeply upset those who hold to traditions and safety. For the young church is indeed beginning to sense its inner meaning and power in ultimate terms, in a spirit of self-sacrifice if necessary, but certainly in terms of imagination, initiative, and attack. Even the Roman Catholic Church was rocked to its heels, during its Second Vatican Council, by the force and steadfastness of young theologians who simply would not capitulate to the Curia and all it stood for in the church: immovability, traditionalism, and the authority of age by merit of age alone.

Granted that Pope John XXIII stimulated the young church there to newness of life, it is becoming more and more clear — even to the secular world — that there resided in the church long before John's papacy that kind of vision, strength, and outreach which needed only freeing to be felt. It is no risk at all to say that this same congealed power awaits freeing and movement in all the churches where the Gospel has been breathed by the Holy Spirit, and we are going to see the freeing and the force of all this in our lifetime—or we are going to see instead such an apostasy from the churches as to shake them further to the roots.

For you cannot frustrate long the power of the Spirit working in youth, even if you try. One way or another, that power will explode into the world and change it, simply because the Holy Spirit is not interested in keeping any church alive just for its own survival or well-being. The youth of the church sense also this thrust toward ultimate goals and so declare their willingness to go the ultimate distance, no matter what the cost.

In possessing this willingness to spend whatever the time and the Spirit call for, the young church finds itself in a new and quite unaccustomed alliance *with* the secular world, not only in Selma and the jails of the South but in Washington, D. C., and the missions of our ambassadors to find a niche of peace in Saigon. Almost overnight the hope of government and the longing of the young church have met after traveling full circle away from each other. For there can be no Gospel in all the world but that the world last long enough for Gospel to be offered everywhere. And I am not so sure how much time we have left.

Neither, of course, is the young person in the church. He is haunted, already in high school years, by an often unconscious sense of destructive power and death in the hands of a man he will never see, sitting at some cold desk in Moscow or Peiping, an array of irrevocable switches before him and no one knows what motives seething inside him. All this is part of the birthright of our Christian teenagers, and from this there will be no freedom in the next century. And the chances are fifty-fifty, as President John F. Kennedy said, that in the next 10 years one of the most diabolical switches may be pulled.

We are all not really as used to living with this birthright as we suppose, and evidence of this is showing up as anxieties not only in ourselves but in our young church. No longer will the old threats of loss of position or of status symbols like cars and homes and yachts or even loss of nervous health and energy suffice to keep a young person inside the value systems of safe society—either inside the church or out of it. For the stakes are too high, the anxiety of youth too intense, and some calamitous abbreviation of life on earth too possible. Preserving the *status quo* is done for as a motivating force with youth, who seem to feel instinctively that the Lord isn't too happy with many things the way they are either.

No wonder we grow so easily upset, then, at the abrupt turnabouts in the youth of the church. For it may be that *we* sense even better than they the impenetrable depth of their restlessness and their commitment, and it may be that we *know* that such desperation can quite possibly lead to utter aloneness and desolation.

I have a friend whose commitment to the church goes only so far as the church is willing to be honest to itself and its mission in the Lord Christ. It is always disturbing for me to talk church with this young man, for I sense in him a lack of those loyalties I was taught to take for granted, a sort of *"my church right or wrong"* attitude that I suppose entered my system with my first breath in the small church parsonage. And now suddenly to confront a devastating integrity so demanding that it will not settle for the consolation of loyalty—how really hard this can be on my acceptance and understanding!

Yet, even for the *sake* of my church, I do not believe I would want to try to change the disturbing limits of this young man's loyalty. Perhaps I sense that only with his kind of reserve will he be able to grow in Christ and His Spirit. And perhaps he can still communicate to me some of that primitive honesty to the Lord that will not allow loyalty to be made a hostage against truth.

For in the most truthful sense of all, the reluctance of my young friend to take to himself the comforts of absolute commitment to a church reveals a faith in the Kingdom of Heaven that is almost vicious in its courage. He is saying to me that the Holy Spirit can do—and perhaps will do—through a single person what we had once assumed He could or would do only through a vast organization of Christians. He is daring to go it alone if that organization at any point becomes less than faith and hope and love require it to be in the world.

What sheer beauty of faith lights the eyes of Christian teen-agers possessed by the courage even to question and counter loyalties to organizations taught them *in the name of Jesus Christ!* What a miracle of the Creator Spirit Himself that a young Christian can by any route at all, even for a moment, transcend the fences built around him by his own heritage and education, built into the psychophysical structures of his own self! How terribly shining with the power and beauty of Christ Himself the face of that girl or boy who cares for our own sake to lift loyalty beyond us to the measureless glory of the throne itself!

It is for this reason, above all, that I have learned to see in our young persons the one majestic hope of the church in this world. They are the letters written to this world in His own hand, and they bear in themselves the marks of His own beauty and grace. And most certainly our world is going to feel the beauty and grace—and power—alive in these young lives! No switch on any desk will move but that their prayers and their courage will move the King of kings who holds that hand in His power.

No Asia or Europe will change the structure of the world but that their growing witness for peace will talk to that force with the force of right and conscience and the fearful dedication possible only for the humble and self-sacrificing.

I see nothing but hope in them, these bright gifts to our spirits. The adventure of our lives will be enhanced by their courage and disregard of danger, their fruits of the faith we have passed on so incompletely to them. That young state senator in my own church may carry his commitment into the White House, and our world will be the better for it. That young pastor's daughter in York may lead the youth program of the young church, and our world will be better for it.

It is possible to faith that our world may even be physically *saved* by these young eyes with their bright vision. If the Lord of creation does choose to prolong the life of our planet, how else would He do it but through the courage and stance of a person of faith in His final significance for this planet? Even our yearning for one world, which balances so fully our yearning for one church, may find realization in the will and work of just one person of faith who may "make the whole difference."

At any rate, as parents and leaders of youth we can experience right now that immense joy of courageous and unreasonable hope in touching the souls of our own young, and in sensing the quiet power of their pulse. We deal not with delinquents but with miracles who will not leave their world the same as they found it. Their love for us is deeper than we think, their commitment to faith richer, and their courage in the world bolder. Even in our frustrations with them, we want to return to a basic confidence in the meaning of their presence with us. For finally, in spite of *our* weaknesses, they may come to see the supporting presence of their King most powerfully in our eyes and in our faces.

And I, for one, would pray that my teen-age daughter might see her Lord in my look at her more than that she might read a dozen books about Him from my pen. Just as you would pray that, by some kindly miracle, you show His love and power and courage to the young around you.

What more would you want to ask, under the mercies of the throne of all heaven?